# VANCOUVER *to* VICTORIA
### Souvenir Guide

# BEAUTIFUL BRITISH COLUMBIA

Published by
*Beautiful British Columbia*
A Division of Great Pacific Industries Inc.

*President:* John L. Thomson
*Director of Publishing:* Tony Owen
*Editor-in-Chief:* Bryan McGill
*Art Director:* Ken Seabrook
*Project Editor:* Rosemary Neering

To order copies of this book call
1-800-663-7611 in Canada or the U.S.
604-384-5456 worldwide.
Fax: 604-384-2812

Beautiful British Columbia
929 Ellery Street
Victoria, B.C.
V9A 7B4

Printed and bound in Vancouver, B.C.
by Quebecor Printing

Colour separations and film
in Vancouver, B.C.
by WYSIWYG Prepress Inc.

**Canadian Cataloguing in Publication Data**
Neering, Rosemary, 1945-
  Vancouver to Victoria

  ISBN 0-920431-27-5
  1. Gulf Islands (B.C.)–Description
and travel.  2. Gulf Islands (B.C.)–
Pictorial works.  I. Beautiful British
Columbia Magazine (Firm) II. Title.
FC3845.G8N43 1995    971.1'2804    C95-910501-8
F1089.G8N43 1995

**A commercial
fishboat heads out at
sunrise for another
working day near
Saltspring Island.**

GUNTER MARX

# CAN THIS BE ROMANCE?

*The Frequent Traveller is reading a newspaper in a corner of the ferry lounge when the Eager Tourist plumps down beside her.*
*"You ride this ship all the time?" asks ET incredulously. "That must be so . . . so," she searches for just the right word, "so romantic."*

*by Rosemary Neering*

Are we on the same ship? Those of us who regularly ride the ferries between the mainland and Vancouver Island have come to regard them simply as transportation, an extension of the highway, but one that forces us to stand in lineups and eat the Sunshine Breakfast. Faced with a first-timer, we're at a bit of a loss. Yes, the scenery is magnificent and the sensations of being at sea quite rejuvenating, but we're just anxious to be on the other side.

And yet . . .

When the captain announces a pod of killer whales is dancing off the port bow, we're the ones pretending to be nonchalant as we sidle over for an unobtrusive look at these formidable, graceful creatures. When the sun slides down behind the Saltspring Island hills and the water turns to silver, we're the ones who suddenly realize we haven't read a page of our books for long minutes. And when the tide rips form off Active Pass or the chop builds on Georgia Strait, only the most jaded among us never poke our noses outside to feel the wind and sun.

So let's admit it: there is something just a touch romantic about travelling between the island and the mainland on one of these imposing vessels, being conveyed through islands that now approach and now recede, catching a glimpse of sea lions and cormorants, crossing a strait where traffic from around the world raises distant silhouettes.

The ferries that now make the 95-minute run between Tsawwassen, south of Vancouver, and Swartz Bay, north of

Victoria, are the inheritors of a long tradition. Back in the days of the Hudson's Bay Company and Fort Victoria, HBC steamers plied from Fort Victoria to Fort Langley, on the Fraser River. When eager gold-rush prospectors flocked to Victoria from 1858 to 1865, they made their way by sea through the Gulf Islands and onto the Fraser.

Even after Vancouver eclipsed Victoria in size and wealth, both cities were part of the triangular Victoria-Vancouver-Seattle run, served by rival steamships from Canadian Pacific and other marine lines.

That perhaps was the time – seen through a retrospective haze – that was the most romantic. Travellers from around the world took ship on this route, lured by its promised beauty. For some, it was less lucky than others. American author Thomas Wolfe – of *Look Homeward Angel* fame – ended his trip to western America in 1938 by sailing from Seattle for Victoria, then taking the *Princess Kathleen* to Vancouver. On board, he fell in with a "poor shivering wretch;" both men drank from the sick man's flask.

CHRIS CHEADLE

above: **ferry passengers in the evening glow.**
left: **a Tsawwassen-Swartz Bay ferry threads its way through Active Pass as a smaller Gulf Islands ferry enters Sturdies Bay, on Galiano Island.** photo: Al Harvey

Was it the flask or was it the fact that Wolfe stayed on deck in a roaring gale to watch the scenery? Whichever, he caught a cold that turned to pneumonia and complications of that disease killed him not many weeks after.

The six-and-a-half-hour run between Victoria and Vancouver harbour is fondly or otherwise remembered by many for whom it was the only way between the cities. By the 1950s, two lines dominated travel between island and mainland: CP and Black Ball ferries. When unions struck both lines in 1958, cutting off the island, the provincial government decided to begin its own service. They had no desire to make the long run; instead, they planned a two-hour shuttle service from south of Vancouver to north of Victoria, between Tsawwassen and Swartz Bay.

Thomas Wolfe wouldn't recognize the service today. Ferries make between 16 and 32 crossings every day, carrying up to 50,000 passengers and some 10,000 vehicles a day at the busiest seasons. A hard-drinking writer might be taken aback at plush chairs, floor-to-ceiling glass, cafeterias with cappuccino, newsstands, video-games emporia, and business cubicles with laptop plug-ins.

But, like both Frequent Traveller and Eager Tourist, he'd still recognize the island shorelines, the shining waves, and the ever-present wildlife – and, like the rest of us, he'd still stand outside in wind or calm to watch this ocean world slip by.

PAUL BAILEY

above: **bald eagles soar above the islands and perch in trees along the ferry route. This eagle occupies an arbutus tree, the picturesque, red-barked, broad-leafed evergreen known elsewhere as the madrona.**

right: **passengers enjoy the sunshine on the ferry deck.** photo: Robert Tompkins

## SPEAKING THE LANGUAGE

Perplexed by seafarers' terms? Can't get your fathoms into cables or your kilometres into knots? Here is a brief guide to sea talk:

**bow:**
the ship's front.

**stern:**
the ship's back.

**port:**
if you are on board, facing the bow, the left side of the ship.

**starboard:**
the right side.

**fathom:**
six feet (1.83 metres).

**cable:**
in Canada, 100 fathoms, 600 feet, 183 metres.

**knot:**
one nautical mile per hour. Never say "10 knots an hour."

**nautical mile:**
1.15 miles, 1.85 kilometres.

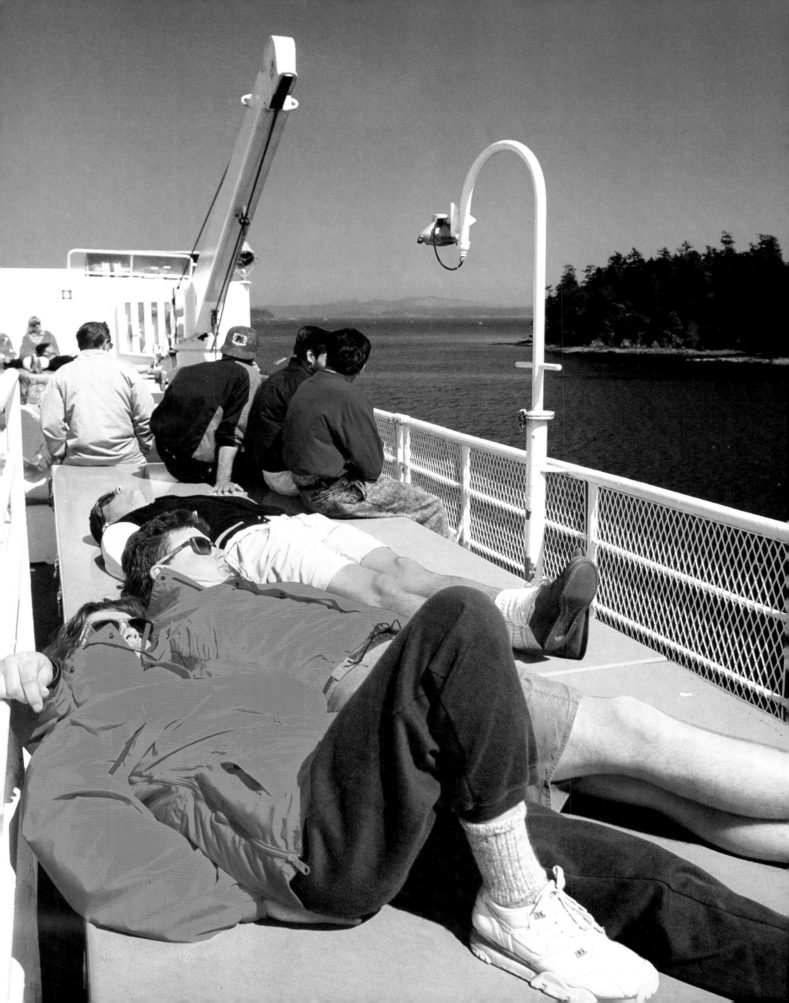

# LEAVING THE MAINLAND

GRAHAM OSBORNE

*Several cars speed up the long causeway, their drivers praying they may still catch this sailing of the* Spirit of Vancouver Island. *But in vain: the bow doors slowly close, and the ship's deep-throated whistle sounds a single long blast. Then the* Spirit *begins to edge astern from the Tsawwassen dock.*

From high on the ship's bridge, which bears an unexpected resemblance to that on the *Starship Enterprise*, a watcher sees the terminal and shoreline as a flat extended line from north to south. To the northwest, a freighter is singling up its lines, preparing to leave Roberts Bank Superport. Every year, 20 million tonnes of coal from mines in western Canada and the U.S. are transferred from 110-car trains to bulk freighters here, for delivery to steel mills across the oceans.

Beside the coal port are the beginnings of a new container terminal, planned to take pressure off the often overloaded Port of Vancouver. Along the shore, waves lap at the shallow mudflats that front the farm fields of the municipality of Delta. These fields are part of the wide, flat delta lands of the Fraser River, formed over millenia by silt and mud swept downriver and deposited at the river's mouth. At the edge of the flats lies Tsawwassen Indian Reserve, site of a new and major condominium development. Tsawwassen is a Coast Salish word, meaning either "facing the sea" or "beach at the mouth."

From where Highway 17 meets the waterfront, a 1.6-kilometre (one-mile) causeway leads to a manmade island. The

## THE TSAWWASSEN BIRDS

Birdwatching at Tsawwassen can help while away time spent in ferry lineups.

Gulls that utter raucous cries as they sweep down on any piece of discarded litter are probably glaucous-winged, the only gulls that breed on the ocean shore. These large white and grey birds, with wingspread up to 1.4 metres, are the best known of local gulls. You may also see the California gull, with grey, black-tipped wings, common in autumn, absent in winter, or the smaller, black-headed Bonaparte's gull. At sea, you're likely to see flocks of mew gulls, smaller and mostly white, feeding along kelp beds and tide rips.

Though gulls are the loudest avian visitors, many other bird species frequent the area near the terminal. Look for various kinds of ducks floating around the docks, especially surf scoters, with distinctive white patches on black heads. Close to shore, north of the terminal, you'll often see long-legged great blue herons stalking tidal flats, bending their long necks down to capture darting minnows or scuttling crabs.

The Fraser delta mudflats, marshes, and farmers' fields form a major staging area for birds migrating in spring and fall, when hundreds of thousands of birds pass through the region.

Snow geese flock to the delta in late September, feeding on the foreshore and on the stubble in fields until December; they return in March. Hundreds of thousands of shorebirds, including huge flocks of western sandpipers, spend time on the delta from mid-April to early May, and from late June to mid-September. Though shorebirds tend to congregate at Boundary Bay, south of the terminal, or at Reifel Bird Sanctuary to the north, out of sight of ferry passengers, flocks may be visible from the terminal.

CAMERON HERYET/T.W.'S IMAGE NETWORK

12 hectares of causeway and island were created in 1958 when the B.C. government chose Tsawwassen, 37 kilometres south of Vancouver, as the mainland terminus for the Victoria-Vancouver ferry service. The terminal has been expanded in the intervening 35 years from one to five docks. Some 2,500 vehicles can line up inside the loading area to wait for ferries bound for Swartz Bay (Victoria), the Gulf Islands, and Nanaimo. Long-time passengers remember the long walk from ticket office to ship, often in rain or wind; foot passengers now reach the ferries by overhead walkways.

To the south, past pleasure boats that anchor out or tie up at buoys protected by causeway and breakwater, the shore curves around a spade-shaped point. In 1846, treaty makers decided that the U.S.-Canada border should follow the 49th parallel as far as the middle of Georgia Strait. The border thus slices across Point Roberts, leaving this squat territory like the American thumbnail on a Canadian thumb.

Its engines astern, the *Spirit* moves out of the dock. Today, winds are light and waves and tides create no problems for the massive ship. The *Spirit's* bridge is 25 metres above the keel; the mast reaches another 18 metres into the sky. It is almost 165 metres long. When storms barrel in with winds of 40 and 45 knots, "the windage on the side of this ship is incredible," says Captain David Myerscough. "That's when you hear about the ferries' tying up," not so much because they cannot dock, but because, plunging with the waves, they cannot load or unload.

"If it's really blowing, we have to slide along this wall," Myerscough points to the side of Dock 1 far below, "and go very slowly, because we're pinned right against it."

As bridge crew watch radar images and check astern, the whistle blasts again and the trip begins.

previous pages: **the berths of the BC Ferry terminal and of Roberts Banks stretch like spider's legs from the causeways that link terminal and port to the Tsawwassen shore.** photo: Steve Short/ First Light

far left: **a western sandpiper pecks at the mudflats; thousands of these small birds visit the Tsawwassen area in spring and fall.**

above: **a freighter loads at the Roberts Bank coal port.**

ROSEMARY NEERING

far left: **the Tsawwassen terminal lies at the end of a man-made causeway. Behind lie the farm fields of Delta, composed of rich silt deposited by the Fraser River over centuries.**
photo: Al Harvey

left: **the caissons and pilings of the Tsawwassen terminal.**

below: **the mouths of the Fraser north of Tsawwassen are home to many a fishing boat, including this buying boat and its companions.**

IMAGES B.C. / T.W.'S IMAGE NETWORK

# STRAIGHT ACROSS THE STRAIT

INFOCUS/JEFF BARBER

previous pages: **orcas slide along the waters of Georgia Strait, with Washington State's Mount Baker to the east.** photo: Chris Cheadle

above: **recreational fishing – mostly for salmon – is a common pastime on both sides of the strait.**

far right: **the Queen of Vancouver heads for the rainbow's end.** photo: Grant Faint

*Scarcely more than two ships' lengths from the Tsawwassen dock, the Spirit crosses the international boundary and enters U.S. waters for 9.5 kilometres. Though ships' crews often joke with inquiring American tourists that the milky, muddy outflow from the Fraser is dirty American water, and the deep clear seawater is clean Canadian water, it's impossible to see where the border lies — unless it is fishing season.*

As salmon return to the Fraser, a major spawning river, in summer and fall, American fishboats crowd close to the boundary, often dropping their nets just into Canadian waters. Ferry captains curse the boundary commission that drew the border out into the strait here, then south through the centre of the strait. They must leave the Tsawwassen dock stern first, swing through a 180-degree turn, then pick their way past fishboats and nets without injuring either.

It can't always be done. When boats are lined up along the border, "I've got two cables [365 metres/1,200 feet] to turn in," says Captain Myerscough; "this ship is almost one cable long. And they're American ships announcing they're in American waters. They aren't going to move." On occasion, a Canadian ferry bow hooks an American fishing net, and damage claims show up on ferry corporation desks.

Fishboats you expect; other traffic near shore can be a surprise. Windsurfers dart out from the sheltered waters behind the causeway, though, in the 1990s, they've almost been replaced by daredevils on jet skis. "They do some very silly things," says Myerscough, "like going across your wash.

They're really pushing their luck. They think it's great fun, and that they're very safe – until the damn thing stops."

The trip across Georgia Strait, here 19 kilometres wide, takes 40 minutes, almost half the crossing time between island and mainland. Georgia Strait is 28 kilometres across at its widest point. It's 222 kilometres long from the U.S.'s San Juan Islands, distantly visible to the southeast, to Quadra and Cortes islands near Campbell River in the north.

Chief steward Catherine Jeffries often tells passengers to spend this time in cafeteria, gift shop, or newsstand, because the ferry won't be close to shore until it has crossed the strait. But, although she has been on this route for 18 years, she still finds time to look out at the water.

"Once you start working with the ships, you're interested in other ships; it's a way of life," she says. "When the car carriers first started coming through here, they were really interesting. And the American aircraft carriers going into Vancouver, they look quite monstrous. Once in a while you see a submarine," heading for Vancouver or for the submarine training base on Vancouver Island's east coast, at Nanoose Bay, "just the

18

conning tower and a little bit of the top of the submarine, steaming along."

Jeffries also likes to trace the brown water spreading out from the Fraser River's mouth, meeting the ocean water. The river sediment has been gathered on the Fraser's 1,368-kilometre journey from the Rocky Mountains to the sea. Once it reaches the

ruffled water that are the surface manifestation of large-scale waves generated underwater. Flotsam and jetsam collect along these unseen crests and troughs, resulting in parallel lines of foam, wood chips, seaweed, and litter.

Thomson also watches waves. Their height depends on wind strength, the length of time the wind has been blowing, and the distance it blows uninterrupted by land. A northerly wind can blow at 40 to 50 knots for several days across the hundred or so kilometres from Texada Island to Tsawwassen. This wind can generate waves up to five metres high, creating stomach-churning conditions aboard the ferry. These and an occasional southeasterly gale, with wind speeds of up to 50 knots, can halt ferry service altogether. But waves of two metres or less, generated by summer northwesterlies or winter southeasterlies, are more common.

For Thomson, every part of the strait is interesting. Big back eddies – whirlpools in the waves – are created near the Tsawwassen terminal as the causeway reflects back currents. Sharp bands of clear and murky water are produced as the ship's propellers churn river and ocean water. Rips – short, steep waves produced when waves meet an opposing current – form at the entrance to Active Pass. These rips are caused by Georgia Strait and Gulf Island water flows meeting and battling each other almost to a standstill.

**Ferry passengers enjoy their sea voyage on deck.**

sea, the runoff forms a plume that spreads southwest, the line between it and the clearer, greener seawater most evident in late spring as snowmelt swells the river.

That runoff is just one feature Rick Thomson sees when he crosses Georgia Strait. An oceanographer with the federal Institute of Ocean Sciences near Victoria, Thomson never tires of watching the water. "On a nice summer day," he says, "you'll see streaky tubes," alternating bands of calm and

Thirty-five minutes out from Tsawwassen, and the bridge crew, relaxed through the strait, once more stands to attention: the ship is approaching Active Pass.

Marine traffic ranges from tiny kayaks to massive freighters. Here, a fishing boat passes the *Queen of Esquimalt*.

# MARINE TRAFFIC

Georgia Strait between the Port of Vancouver and the Strait of Juan de Fuca is one of the busiest waterways on the Pacific coast. That's because it is the main route between American Puget Sound, Juan de Fuca Strait , Vancouver, and points north on island and mainland. Among the marine traffic you may see:

**Deep-sea freighters:** container ships, with characteristic deck cranes used to load and unload boxcar-shaped containers; bulk freighters, which fill their holds with cargoes such as coal or wheat; other ships with cargo in the holds or on deck.

**Ferries:** BC Ferries sail from Tsawwassen for Swartz Bay, the Gulf Islands, and Nanaimo. They're recognizable by their colour scheme (white with blue and red trim), and their bow and stern doors that open to load vehicles.

**Cruise** ships: sleek in silhouette, often painted white, with rows of windows and portholes on passenger decks. Usually destined for Vancouver, Victoria, and, eventually, Alaska by way of the Inside Passage north along the B.C. coast.

**Fishboats:** seiners and trawlers carry net drums near the stern. Trollers are the smallest fishboats, carrying long poles with fishlines attached. If the poles are standing at attention, the boat is not fishing; if the poles are at a 45-degree angle, the boat is looking for a catch.

**Navy ships:** aircraft carriers, submarines, warships, from Canada, the United States, and other nations.

**Tugs and tows:** tugboats, with high bows that slope down to a low stern. Tows range from barges loaded with containers, houses, logs, or anything else a customer wants moved up or down the coast, to log booms, though these are now fairly rare. You may have to look well astern of a tug to finds its tow; tow lines are long to permit easy manoeuvring and stopping.

# ACTIVE PASS

ROBERT TOMPKINS

On the bridge, Second Mate Alec Scoones announces on the distress frequency — monitored by all ships — that the Spirit of Vancouver Island is off the Gossip Point buoy, southbound through Active Pass. He has already called Vancouver traffic to find out if there are other ships in the vicinity. The steering has been switched from automatic to manual, and the engine room is standing by.

previous pages: **a pleasure cruiser and the giant *Spirit of British Columbia* leave Active Pass on their way to Georgia Strait.** photo: Gunter Marx

above: **great blue herons are among the birds that frequent the shallows along the shorelines.**

far right: **sunset at Montague Harbour, on Galiano Island.** photo: Paul Bailey

Active Pass, a dogleg with blind turns, is the main route between Georgia Strait and Gulf Island waters. A glance at the map shows it provides the most direct passage between southern Vancouver Island and the Lower Mainland and permits the ferries to maintain a two-hour shuttle service.

The pass demands respect: ferries, pleasure boats, fishboats, tugs and tows, and the occasional freighter sail its narrow confines, dealing with currents and tides that rush between its island walls. Five hundred and fifty to 1,700 metres wide, with two right-angle turns, it is the most navigationally difficult part of the voyage between Tsawwassen and Swartz Bay.

Each ferry crew sails the 5.5-kilometre pass four times a day, up to 200 days a year. But no one takes anything for granted: this deep and narrow passageway has claimed its victims in the past, and the ferries are not immune. In 1970, near the pass's south entrance, the Soviet freighter *Sergei Yesenin* sliced into the side of the *Queen of Victoria*, killing three passengers and causing $1 million in damage. This was the worst accident in BC Ferries' history.

The pass is also the most scenic stretch of the Tsawwassen-Swartz Bay route. Of necessity, the ferries sail close to the shores of Mayne and Galiano islands, and passengers get their closest look at land.

Schools of herring congregate at the entrances to the pass, attracting salmon that return through here on their way to spawn in the Fraser River. The marine life in turn attracts birds, ranging from gulls and ungainly, black cormorants to thousands of Arctic loons and hundreds of bald eagles that migrate through the area in March. Orcas (killer whales), sea lions, and seals are more often seen in and at the entrances to Active Pass than on any other part of the ferry trip.

The name "Active" should surely stem from all the activity here; in fact, it results from some gentle but determined diplomacy. Though most of the geographic points in this area are named for 19th-century British survey ships, their crew and their friends, and sundry British noblemen back home, Active Pass was named by the captain of the U.S. survey ship *Active*, sailing these waters just before a British ship arrived. The British captain agreed to let the name stand, but, suspecting the Americans might be claiming territory as much as

previous pages: **seen from above, the Georgina Point lighthouse on Mayne Island warns sea traffic of the dangers at the eastern entrance to Active Pass.** photo: The Russ Heinl Group

right: **the bow doors on the ferry that serves Mayne Island.**

below: **kayakers paddle along the shore near Galiano's Montague Harbour.**

DAVID NUNUK

naming it, "I have at the same time fully explained to him [the *Active's* captain] that the gift of naming all places on our side rests solely with us."

The *Active*, by the way, lived up to a former name of *Goldhunter*: when the ship returned to San Francisco in 1858, the crew carried the news of gold found on the Fraser River sandbars that triggered the gold rush.

Two lights mark the Georgia Strait

entrance to the pass. To the northwest, the Gossip Shoals light (a green buoy) and fog bell warn of dangers off Gossip Island. Regrettably, the origin of the name Gossip is uncertain. While some suggest it refers to the murmuring of water on the shoals, others to the murmuring of the islanders, both heard from neighbouring Galiano, neither explanation seems likely.

To the southeast, the red and white Georgina Point lighthouse on Mayne Island blinks its warning. Georgina Point was the Gulf Islands' first lighthouse, built in 1885. Not long after transplanted Shetland Islander Henry "Scotty" Georgeson became the light's first keeper, he requested a horn or fog bell, since fog often veiled the island's shores. He got his foghorn in 1889; he continued to man the light until 1920, witnessing the 1918 accident, when the CPR steamer *Princess Adelaide* grounded on the rocks, where it remained for three days.

The 11-metre-tall tower houses a light that is visible for almost 20 kilometres. Beyond the lighthouse stretch the serried ranks of hills that form Mayne and Saturna islands.

The ferry passes Sturdies Bay on Galiano, location of that island's ferry terminal. Alec Scoones gestures toward a land feature beyond the bay, not named for an early explorer. His grandfather and great-uncle pioneered nearby, where they and Scoones's grandmother held musical evenings around their bamboo-needled gramophone – which the family still owns. Many points and bays on these islands are named after pioneers.

The ship's whistle sounds its deep warning again as the ferry angles around the first blind turn, off Galiano's Mary Anne Point. Though the ship passes close to land here, Scoones notes that there is very little danger. "It's very deep – from 90 metres off Helen Point to 80 in Miners Bay," to 20 metres at its shallowest point. "You could drive the ship right up and hit the visible part of the land before anything else." These deep waters make it possible for two ferries to pass abreast in Active Pass, a common occurrence, because the pass marks the halfway point between Tsawwassen and Swartz Bay.

**The tugboat *Seaspan Navigator* chugs through the narrows of Active Pass.**

29

## SEA LIONS AND SEALS

As the ferry edges around Helen Point, passengers often catch sight of odd-shaped driftwood lying on the rocks. Then one of the pieces barks, and raises itself on shiny wet flippers, part of a lounging colony of sea lions.

Twenty years ago, you could be fairly sure that these were northern or Steller's sea lions, mammals that weigh up to a tonne and measure as long as three metres. Some 20 of B.C.'s 6,000 Steller's spend the winter here, catching fish, resting on the rocks, and letting loose with their distinctive, rasping bark.

But in the last two decades, California sea lions – the animals that show up in circuses and aquaria, balancing balls on their heads – have moved into this territory. They're smaller and darker than their northern cousins, a difference often difficult to see from the deck of a ferry – though you *could* throw one a ball . . .

Along the rocks or in the water near land, you may also see harbour seals. Short-flippered and much smaller than sea lions, these sea mammals are most often spotted by their whiskered noses and appealing eyes breaking the waterline as they come up to breathe. Seals can stay underwater for as long as 20 minutes, though five to six minutes is more usual.

Opposite Mary Anne Point, on Mayne Island, is the deep curve of Miners Bay. In 1858 and 1859, prospectors on their way from Victoria to the mainland and the Fraser River gold rush found the bay a convenient stopping place before they entered the open waters of Georgia Strait. Later, as steamers made the regular run between Victoria and Vancouver, they too stopped at Miners Bay, dropping off mail and supplies for all the Gulf Islands. Mayne Island became a popular holiday and excursion spot.

The ferry makes its second right-angled turn around Helen Point, on Mayne Island. This land is a Coast Salish reserve, one of several on the Gulf Islands. Archaeologists have dated material found here back 3,000 years. The Coast Salish used Gulf Island beaches as campsites, where they could fish, dig for clams, and smoke seafood over fires.

Those who sail at night often see a light signalling from the Galiano shore opposite Helen Point. "We knew a lot of the skippers on the Gulf Islands ferries," says Betty Kennedy of herself and her husband Gilbert, who have spent their weekends on Galiano for 32 years. "Most of them moved up to the bigger ferries. They used to wave at us when they came through, and we'd wave back. At night, we'd use a flashlight."

When the *Sergei Yesenin* crashed into the *Queen of Victoria*, the Kennedys were in the boat closest to the accident. Their testimony helped show that the freighter's pilot was most at fault. "Since then, we've been handed on from one set of crew to another, and almost all of them wave." The original story has been lost and few crew members now know who the Kennedys are. Last year, a crew member told Kennedy, "We've been waving to people on that point for years and years, and we have no idea who they are."

As they round Helen Point, ferry crew keep an especially close lookout for small boats. The entrances to Active Pass are

## A CORRIDOR OF BALD EAGLES

The bald eagle may be miscast as the symbol of the U.S. It's endangered in the lower 48 states, but thriving along British Columbia's coast.

Some 100 pairs of bald eagles nest in the Gulf Islands, many in eyries on the Active Pass shoreline of Mayne Island. Up to several hundred of the 30,000 bald eagles that winter on the B.C. coast spend time here.

Look for their white heads or their raptors' silhouettes atop the tallest trees, watching for prey such as gulls, ducks, or fish swimming near the surface.

Prey spotted, they plummet to the water to grasp fish or fowl in their talons.

Young eagles are brown and mottled white. The birds develop the white head and tail that makes them unmistakable when they are four to five years old.

THE RUSS HEINL GROUP

among the best spots in the Gulf Islands for salmon fishing. Fishermen boat in, set their hooks and wait, often trolling slowly across Helen Point and directly into the path of ferries that have established routes and long stopping distances.

"You get 50 or more fishboats right across here sometimes," says Scoones. "To us, they look very close; to them we're a big boat. They kind of move at a different pace, or sometimes they refuse to move. The

RCMP go out and move them away. Sometimes they'll say, `Could the ferry just wait? I've got a big one on the line.' I don't know what they're thinking – or maybe they're just not thinking."

The dogleg past, the ferry skirts the floating kelp and white, red-banded light that mark Enterprise Reef, off Mayne's Village Bay and the island's ferry terminal, to enter the third stage of the journey.

above: **Saturna Island lies beyond the ferry route, the easternmost Canadian Gulf Island.**

far left: **sea lions stare curiously from shoreline rocks.**

33

# THE GULF ISLANDS

GUNTER MARX

*The ferry leaves Active Pass and Galiano Island behind. Mayne Island lies to port; to starboard, Prevost Island fronts the hills that rise to low mountains on Saltspring. Saturna Island is briefly visible at the end of the channel between Mayne and North Pender; ahead are Portland and Moresby islands.*

These and other smaller neighbouring isles are part of the Gulf Islands, a grouping that lies in the Strait (originally named the Gulf) of Georgia between Vancouver Island and the mainland.

They bear a definite family resemblance. Ages ago, glaciers scraped valleys between sandstone ridges, and created fingerlike points that trend northwest-southeast, the direction of the glaciers' travel. The points and ridges are often visible from the ferry.

Galiano presents the most evident example, for the entire island is a long narrow ridge, 26 kilometres long and no more than a few kilometres wide. The Galiano Bluffs, about halfway along the island's Active Pass shoreline, are fine examples of the wind-and-wave eroded cliffs common on the islands. Waves have also worn away at glacial deposits, forming characteristic rounded bays.

Climate and vegetation underscore the islands' family resemblance. In the rain shadow of Vancouver Island, the Gulf Islands are on average sunnier and drier than neighbouring areas of either Vancouver Island or the mainland. Ferry travellers can see Douglas-fir forests, which thrive in this climate, and clusters of arbutus and Garry oak, both of which grow in Canada only here and on Vancouver Island's east coast.

Transportation to the islands is by ferry or private boat. This relative isolation has encouraged an independent yet relaxed lifestyle. Each island has developed its own version of that lifestyle. Galiano is known as the home of artists and writers, as well as fervent and successful battlers against development. Mayne is home to some subdivisions, but also to turn-of-the-century mansions.

Saturna, visible to port as the ferry leaves Mayne Island behind, was on the route of the Spanish naval schooner *Saturnina* in 1791, and thus acquired its name. Officers of that same ship, incidentally, named the nearby strait the *Gran Canal de Nuestra Senora del Rosario de la Marinera*. Surveyors who renamed it the Strait of Georgia in honour of King George III have been thanked by later generations of mapmakers.

More isolated than most, the 250 or so Saturna islanders are content to live a self-sufficient lifestyle that is under threat elsewhere on the Gulf Islands.

West of the ferry route south of Active Pass lies Prevost Island, identifiable by the Portlock Point lighthouse, a squat white-shingled tower. Prevost was bought in 1924 by Irish immigrant Digby Hussey de Burgh. Some of his descendants still live there.

Behind Prevost is Saltspring, the largest and most populous Gulf Island at 180

previous pages: **waves wash into the campground at Ruckle Provincial Park on Saltspring Island as an outbound ferry passes by.** photo: Gunter Marx

above: **kayaks bring colour to a marina at North Pender Island's Otter Bay.**

far right: **one of the ferries that link Saltspring Island to Vancouver Island approaches harbour.** photo: Jeff Barber\INFocus

previous pages:
**seen from the air, the long narrow hills of Prevost Island display the glacial scouring that shaped this and many other Gulf Islands.** photo: The Russ Heinl Group

above: **cooking crab on an campfire is a Gulf Island tradition.**

above far right: **orcas knife through the water.**

square kilometres and 7,500 residents. The only island with hospital, high school, and other amenities, Saltspring is attracting more and more people and more and more developers. It's the scene of constant battles between those who want to retain their relatively rural lifestyle and those who yearn for condominiums, marinas, and profit.

The highest points on the Gulf Islands are on Saltspring. Mounts Tuan, Bruce, and Baynes – which islanders insist on calling Mount Maxwell – reach to 700 metres. If conditions are right and your eyes keen, you may sight hang-gliders who soar with the updrafts near these mountains. Perhaps the most easily identifiable feature on Saltspring's shoreline is Beaver Point, where colourful tents often cluster near Ruckle Provincial Park beach.

Across the channel from Prevost and Saltspring, North Pender Island was once linked to South Pender by a low neck of land. But, frustrated by the long distance they had to travel by boat to go from one shore to the other, pioneer residents convinced government to dredge a canal across the land neck. Predictably, the two islands thus created were rejoined by a highway bridge in 1955.

The northernmost sculpted bay on Pender's coast is Grimmer Bay – not grimmer because of some horrific tragedy at sea, but for early settler Washington Grimmer, who built the Penders' first steamer wharf.

The Pender ferry terminal at Otter Bay is visible in the next bay, about halfway along the shore. It's a common story – almost a legend now – among ferry crew that they often see bears north of Otter Bay. That would be "bares," or sunbathing women who wave at passing ships. Otter Bay is more legitimately remembered as the site of a herring saltery run by Japanese Canadians who were exiled from the coast and interned during the Second World War.

If you look across the channel from Otter Bay, you can see the entrance to Ganges Harbour; Ganges, at the head of the harbour, is Saltspring's largest town.

A housing development on Pender that greatly influenced the Gulf Islands can't be seen from the ferries. In the 1960s and 1970s, developers turned part of North Pender into suburbia with a subdivision called Magic Lake Estates. Horrified by the thought that all the Gulf Islands might be developed in this way, Gulf Islanders banded together to demand action from the provincial government. The result, the Islands Trust, with elected representatives from the 13 islands it includes, sits in judgment over development and zoning.

As they leave Swanson Channel, the Penders and Saltspring behind, the ferries take different routes to Swartz Bay. The smaller *Queens* sail west of Portland Island, the larger *Spirits* between Portland and Moresby.

## ORCA: THE "KILLER" WHALE

Perhaps no sight more entrances ferry passengers than that of a pod of shimmering black orcas leaping and curving through Georgia Strait or Gulf Island waters.

These much-studied marine mammals are toothed whales. Their non-scientific name, killer whales, was no doubt bestowed by early observers who saw them surround and kill porpoises, catch sea lions in their jaws, or tear flesh from the bodies of larger whales.

Researchers can now prove that each whale can be identified by the white markings on its back and belly and by the shape of its dorsal fin. Many orcas belong to pods, groups of five to 50, that stay together throughout their lives. Male orcas can reach 11 metres in length, with dorsal fins up to three metres high, and weigh as much as 10 tonnes. They reach speeds of 50 kilometres an hour as they slice through the water.

The orcas you see on this route are probably part of a J, K, or L pods, about 100 resident whales that stay year-round in these waters, feeding mostly on salmon. Transient whales also pass through the area; they feed mostly on other marine mammals.

Orcas are most commonly seen at the entrances to Active Pass, though they may show up anywhere in Gulf Island waters.

right: **boats at Port Washington on North Pender island.**

far right: **an arbutus tree warmed by sunlight on a rocky island shore.** photo: Duncan McDougall.

## ARBUTUS: THE BROAD-LEAFED EVERGREEN

Standing close to the shore or silhouetted on rocky headlands on Portland and many other Gulf Islands are arbutus trees, the shiny-leafed, red-barked trees that are Canada's only broad-leafed evergreens.

The tree is formally named *arbutus menziesii* for Archibald Menzies, naturalist and surgeon who sailed with Captain George Vancouver in the late 18th century. In the United States, it is known as madrona, a name given by Spanish explorers.

It is unlike any other northwest tree. Its shredding bark reveals new pale green or rusty red bark. Its dark glossy leaves are joined by clusters of white flowers in spring and by reddish-orange berries in fall. Its trunks are many and curved: they rise to the crown of leaves, creating a distinctive silhouette.

Though the Coast Salish ate the berries and made spoons from the roots, the arbutus now has little commercial use, for though its grain is beautiful, the dense wood is difficult to cut.

Moresby is probably the largest B.C. island in single private hands. Sold in 1975 for almost $3 million, it is worth perhaps ten times that amount now. But John Elliott remembers an earlier Moresby. When he was nine years old, his parents moved the family from Saturna to Moresby, where they rented farmland. From the age of 16 to 19, Elliott lived alone on the island. "You did things on your own devices," he recalls, "and the best thing was the simplicity of life. People would come to visit, and the first few days they'd wander around saying how lucky you were. Then they'd ask, 'Well, when are you going to town?' and you'd say, 'Well, maybe next Wednesday.'" Few visitors lasted long after that.

Elliott's family also pastured sheep on Portland Island, across the channel, until the government acquired the island. Then, in what he thought was a symbolic gesture, Premier W.A.C. Bennett handed Portland over to Princess Margaret when she visited B.C. in 1958, expecting her to donate it back as a park. But, says Elliott, "she said, 'Well, now I'm a B.C. landowner,' and went back home. It wasn't being used, and we didn't see any reason we couldn't keep sheep on it, so we wrote to her, and her secretary wrote back that she couldn't see any reason either. We probably had the only sheep in B.C. [pastured] by royal assent."

When the princess did return the island to the province in 1967, it was declared a marine park. Princess Margaret Marine Park, 180 hectares in size, attracts pleasure boaters, including kayakers and canoeists, to its white sand beaches and park trails.

As the *Spirit* curves past Portland Island, crew member Glen Brown spots a square-bowed shallow-draft landing craft that serves as part of the inter-island transportation system. Though ferries serve the larger islands, residents of the smaller islands must devise their own ways of moving themselves and their possessions.

Bob Cutting's company has the contract to deliver propane, gas, and potable water to some of the small islands. His tug, *Demac II*, tows a barge that can carry up to 140 tonnes of cargo, on a weekly freight run. That freight ranges from gas and water to refrigerators, stoves, drainage rock, vehicles – "anything people need on a water-access island." The tug approaches the drop point, the crew lets the towline go, and the barge slides onto the beach, and drops a ramp. Cutting also has a new landing craft that he'll use for smaller jobs.

"We'll do everything no one else wants to do," he says. "We take anything that's too wide, too high, or too heavy to go any other way."

Across the channel, the Saltspring shore cuts back into a deep bay. Fulford Harbour, at the head of the bay, is the most used of the island's three ferry terminals. Ahead of the ferry appears the entrance to Swartz Bay. As the Gulf Islands fall astern, the last word on their lifestyle and the changes that face it goes to John Elliott, who comments caustically on newcomers: "People come to the islands and fancy themselves Gulf Islanders. Then they get upset if the ferry's 10 minutes late."

# ARRIVING ON VANCOUVER ISLAND

The cluster of islands north of Swartz Bay guards three possible passages into and out of the ferry terminal. Inbound, the larger *Spirits* leave Moresby Passage for Colburne Passage between Coal and Pym and Knapp islands. The *Queens* follow the passage between Knapp and Piers Island both in and outbound. Outbound, the *Spirits* sail west, then north, skirting Arbutus and Piers islands.

previous pages: **the *Spirit of British Columbia*, seen here from Canoe Cove, heads towards its Swartz Bay dock.**
photo: Chris Cheadle

KARL SPREITZ

above: **island dwellers improvise to get goods to cottage or home.**

far right: **ferry wash and the Swartz Bay terminal.**
photo: Trevor Bonderud

Captain George Richards, commanding the survey ship HMS *Plumper* in 1858, named Pym, Knapp, and Piers islands for fellow naval officers. But you will look in vain for a Richards Island: an English officer and gentleman could not name anything after himself. Of the three whose names were preserved here, Knapp has the most idiosyncratic claim to fame: a naval instructor, he could draw a perfect circle instantly and unaided by mechanical means, then accurately place a dot on the exact centre. You won't see the ghost of naval surgeon Henry Piers on his island, but you may see signs of a previous name: native people knew this as Crow Island.

Piers Island, the largest of the three at 96 hectares, has had its moments. Bought by English gentleman adventurer Clive Phillipps-Wolley in about 1900, it provided insufficient excitement for its swashbuckling owner, who sold it to a grandson of coal magnate Robert Dunsmuir. He in turn resold it to a syndicate that built a hotel, which promptly and suspiciously burned down. Leased to sheep grazers, Piers was later expropriated by the B.C. government and used as a detention camp for Sons of Freedom Doukhobors convicted of arson in B.C.'s West Kootenay region. Eventually developers bought and subdivided it. Homeowners now commute to Swartz Bay by boat.

Their boats and others can bring both anxiety – if they speed across the ferry's path – and amusement for ferry crews. Captain David Myerscough has seen a few strange sights in his years at sea, but none so strange as here: a full-grown Siberian tiger lazing on

the prow of a sleek motorboat gunning across the channel. Crew members later discovered the tiger was the pet and prop of a stripper appearing at a Victoria hotel.

As it nears the terminal, the ferry makes a wide turn that brings it stern first into harbour. When the government decided to operate BC Ferries in 1958, they chose Swartz Bay, 32 kilometres north of Victoria and then just a little dock at the end of a dirt road, as the island terminus. The highway was extended, and the terminal built. It now houses five docks; these larger ferries use docks 1 and 2, where vehicle loading ramps are widest and have the heaviest load limits.

A recent $4.5-million revamping has greatly improved foot passenger facilities. Some 565 cars can line up in the 12 Swartz Bay-Tsawwassen lanes of the terminal lot, with another 11 lanes reserved for over-height and commercial vehicles.

Vehicles and passengers bound for Victoria disembark here – at least most of them do. Chief steward Catherine Jeffries has had more than a few foot passengers approach her after the ship leaves Swartz Bay on its return trip to Tsawwassen. "What time do we get to Victoria?" they ask, leaving Jeffries at a loss for a suitable answer.

From here, it's a five-minute drive to Sidney, with its new marina facilities, or a half-hour trip to downtown Victoria.

above: **purple and ochre sea stars grip rocks along the shore.**

right: **cormorants perch atop Swartz Bay pilings.**

JANET DWYER

## PILINGS, CAISSONS AND BARNACLES

As the ship enters dock at Swartz Bay, it grazes gently against pilings whose tar-black colour and encrusted barnacles would have you believing these are stalwart old wooden posts.

But they're not. Although pilings at some docks that serve the smaller Gulf Island ferries are wooden, those at berths 1 and 2 are black-painted steel, socketed into the rock that forms the Swartz Bay sea floor.

The pilings spear through the 15 to 20 metres (50 to 60 feet) of water at Swartz Bay. Protecting them are multi-coloured fenders, which are highly visible from the car deck as the ferry gentles into its berth. Made of a special type of shock-absorbing material, these V-shaped supports slow the vessel without rocking it or the berth.

Is Tsawwassen the same? "Swartz Bay is a cakewalk compared to Tsawwassen," says Gary Gawdin of BC Ferries capital works division. "Tsawwassen is much more skookum, because of the weather problems and the open strait." At Tsawwassen, steel caissons filled with concrete and gravel lie alongside the steel pilings, which must be driven another nine metres (30 feet) into the sandy soil that forms the sea bottom around the Fraser River delta.

As for those barnacles, Gawdin says they play no favourites: they'll grow on wood, steel or any other substance they can get their hooks into.

KARL SPREITZ

**A passenger looks out over Swanson Channel as the ferry nears Swartz Bay.**

## GREENING OF THE FERRIES

"Follow the birds to Vancouver Island," tourism operators advertised as early as the 1930s. What they neglected to say was that the seagulls following the ships that plied the Vancouver-Victoria route were attracted by galley garbage thrown overboard.

Few gulls fly in the wake of ships these days. BC Ferries forbids the tossing overboard of a single piece of garbage, and the new *Spirit*-class ships are vessels as green as you'll find anywhere in the world.

Each ship has two sewage treatment plants on board, one fore, one aft. Within the tanks, bacteria, some natural and some added, digest human waste from the heads and organic matter from the galleys. This produces a clear effluent that then goes through an ultraviolet sterilizer.

Non-organic waste from the ships is compacted and removed to landfills after the ship docks. Recycling bins on the ships take newsprint, cardboard, and aluminum cans, and BC Ferries no longer accepts products in glass bottles.

The *Spirits'* engines run at a constant rpm, releasing few pollutants into the air. Variable-pitch propellers soften changes in the ships' speed.

But decisions made to benefit the environment are rarely simple. Rob Hamilton, BC Ferries environmental coordinator, notes that the corporation changed several years ago from heavy foam cups to paper ones. Then almost everyone started to double cup to keep the coffee from burning their hands.

The corporation eventually found a thin-wall Styrofoam cup blown with $CO_2$, so manufacturing produces no greenhouse gases. Wherever possible, washable cups are used. BC Ferries hopes to introduce a commuter mug that will save travellers money and the corporation dishwashing.

# SHIPS OF THE LINE

If you take a ferry between Tsawwassen and Swartz Bay, you will probably be riding on one of six ships: The S-class *Spirit of British Columbia* or *Spirit of Vancouver Island*, or the V-class *Queen of Victoria, Queen of Vancouver, Queen of Esquimalt*, or *Queen of Saanich*.

Some data about the two types of ships:

## THE SPIRITS:

**length:** 167.5m (560 ft).

**depth below the waterline:** 5m (16.5 ft).

**displacement:** 11,609 metric tonnes when loaded.

**seating:** 1,000 in three lounges; 300 in cafeteria; 380 on outside decks.

**maximum passenger load:** 2,100, passengers and crew.

**vehicle capacity:** up to 470 cars, depending on type. Maximum vehicle height, 4.6m (15 ft.).

**bridge:** fully enclosed with computerized navigation systems. Bridge wings extend over the water on either side of the ship; floor-to-ceiling windows, and windows in the floor on the bridge wings give clear 180° views.

**engines:** two drive shafts, each with two six-cylinder, four-stroke diesel engines.

**propellers:** highly skewed, controllable pitch; high lift flap rudders.

**service speed:** 19.5 knots.

**construction:** built in 1991-94, at a cost of approximately $130 million each.

## THE QUEENS:

**built:** 1962 or 1963, in Victoria or Vancouver shipyards, with a capacity of 100 cars. In the late '60s and early '70s, platform decks and midsections were added to the ships. In 1981, each ship was carefully sliced apart horizontally, just below the present promenade deck, the superstructure lifted, and an additional car deck added. There is some variation in size between ships.

**length:** 130m (426 ft).

**gross tonnage:** 9,294 to 9,357.

**car capacity:** 286 to 376.

**passenger capacity:** 1,360.

**service speed:** 19 knots

A V-class *Queen* sails through Gulf Island waters.
photo: Jeff Barber/INFocus